How to Be an Attractive Woman

A Step by Step Method for Becoming Everything a Man Wants and Everything Your Competition Doesn't Want You to Be!

Table of Contents

Thank you!

Thank you for buying this book!

If you enjoy the book and get some value from it, I would appreciate if you could **leave an honest review** on the Amazon store after finishing.

Thank you and enjoy the book!

***

Receive updates on new book releases, book promotions and much more from Niel Schreiber by signing up to the e-mail list: **http://bit.ly/bonus_schreiber_cs**

***

Follow us, Lean Stone Publishing, the publishing company that published this book. You will receive information on upcoming book launches, free book promotions and much more. Sign up to this e-mail list: **http://bit.ly/list_lsp_cs**

***

Like us at **www.facebook.com/leanstonepublishing**

Follow us on Twitter **@leanstonebooks**

Introduction

Hello, again!

Welcome back to the Schreiber School of Social Niceties!

Today I want to start off by both thanking you and congratulating you for downloading the book, "How to Be an Attractive Woman - A Step by Step Method for Becoming Everything a Man Wants and Everything Your Competition Doesn't Want You to Be!"– With the wave of feminism that seems to be sweeping through this 'modern world' it is very easy for women to find that they have lost the ability to balance their independence with their ability to project attractiveness to the opposite sex. Because let's face facts, no matter what they say, this trend of rainbow colored armpit hair and ham-fisted mannerisms is not what men are looking for.

Since you have downloaded this, you probably already know what it feels like to be considered unattractive in the eyes of the men you want. However, rest assured your situation is merely temporary. For years' women across the world have been trying to understand exactly what it is that men find so irresistible in the Kate Upton's of the world. That search ends today.

This book is about to show you what you need to understand about attraction in terms of your man, but also what your man wants to see in you. What is it about certain women that make them so attractive to men? What is it that causes that magnetic pull?

Keep reading, you have come to the right place, just remember that a man's world is governed by the 5 A's of attraction. And this book is about to tell you exactly how you can develop each of those factors so they apply to you.

Thanks once again for buying this book, I hope you enjoy it!

Chapter 1 - The Five A's of Attraction

To start with, the first thing we need to understand is the role 'Attraction' plays in the lives of women, how it does or doesn't impact the way they see themselves, and how the world sees them as well. Unfortunately, as chauvinistic as it may sound, appearance plays a large role in attraction in regards to women, it always has and it probably always will. However, while that is an undeniable truth, it is just as true that attraction, contrary to popular opinion, is about a lot more than simply looking pretty. Attraction is triggered by confidence, composure, character, and personality, all of which culminate to form the magnetic animal pull that a person has. For women, all of this is packaged together with feminine notions of fragility, and delicacy, which in conjunction bring out the protective instincts of men.

You see ladies, we men are simple minded creatures – and while most of us are all for female empowerment, fighting about every little thing is really not our idea of a good time.

Let me see if I can explain this to you, sometimes the things you may see as chauvinistic, are really just us trying to express how we feel about you.

For instance:

We like being able to protect you; that does not mean we don't think you are not already a strong independent lady – it simply makes us feel better about our role. It may be a bit of 'Tarzan and Jane' but it is true nonetheless. But that is just us – if you want to know the things *we* find attractive in a woman on a more 'personality check' level, keep reading, cause I'm about to talk you through that as well.

Just remember that you want to be as open-minded about these things as possible, for many of you these will have to be adapted to fit your personality to a certain extent so keep that in mind. Also keep in mind that you are doing this for yourself and not for us men – no matter what the title of this book says.

Seriously!

You have to want to incorporate these changes for yourself – otherwise they are always just going to be a façade and façades break eventually. This has to be real, it may take some time, and it may be a slow process – but don't just use this list as an 'Acting Skills Guide Book' – use it as 'Chicken Soup for your Future Love Life' - you won't regret it!

Now, in this book, we are going to start off by listing five factors that define the notion of attractiveness as they pertain to women. I want you to remember that this isn't a strict set of rules, think of it more as a step by step guide to the behavior patterns which you Ladies need to adapt if you are to make yourselves more attractive to the opposite sex.

Each of these chapters deals with a different aspect of female behavior, how it is generally viewed by men, and how you can change that aspect through specific guidelines, to ensure that is more in line with the generally preferred method – and by preferred we mean by us men of course.

Now as an example let's start with the 'Approach' – how can a woman best approach a man without coming off as desperate or needy? Trust me Ladies, this one is a winner – master this and you won't have to wait for the desperados to come drop you a pickup line – you can do your own thing – and you can do it with panache!

Is your pulse racing already? Great!

Now think of this - How can 'Amiability' help back up this unforeseen approach tactic? Basically how can you back up your smooth approach? We'll even go into 'Activity' – and what can a woman actively do to make herself more attractive. Think about it, are there certain activities she can engage in to make herself more 'attractive'? If so what are they and how do they help?

Thing is it doesn't stop there – now that we've gotten into the whole sexual attraction thing – let's try this - what about physical attraction?

How can a woman make herself more physically appealing to a man?

What should she wear or refrain from wearing?

Are there any changes she needs to make to her daily regimen? And moving on from physical attraction let's talk about the woman's personality. How assertive do men prefer their women to be?

How can women be assertive without being pushy and how can they be submissive without coming off as weak willed?

Is your head spinning because you've just realized you have no clue how to answer any of those questions?

Well stop worrying!

This book covers all of this and more as we discuss each of these factors in depth, and then show you how to become the woman every man dreams of and every woman wants to be!

Chapter 2 - Approach

The rule of thumb for most cases, as it pertains to male-female interaction, is that women are not the predators. In other words, women do not approach men. The reasoning behind this seemingly quixotic notion of a woman's place actually comes from detailed in depth study of the male psyche.

You see dear reader, from time immemorial, man has been the hunter, the provider and as such the selector. As such, this right of selection has not only been ingrained in his very DNA, but it is also intricately involved with how he views the female sex.

We men are simply programmed to think that it's our job to do the whole approach the girl thing. Think of it like this, a male in his prime will always view the female of his species as fragile and in need of protection. This notion, however backdated, is what brings out the sense of proprietorship in a man, as well as his sense of duty. As an Alpha it is his job to provide you with security and that sense of safety you have been yearning for.

You know how you love it when a man is protective of you, or even when he does something as simple as pull back a chair or open a door, that is what he's thinking – which is exactly why you are going to need to be as delicate as you can when it comes to the approach technique – you want him to feel like it's his idea.

You see while I may understand that not all women have the luxury of waiting around for a man to notice them so that they can pander to their primitive sense of ownership, that bit is still ingrained in men. This is why women today need to be much subtler in how they deal with men. The key to understanding and executing the perfect approach lies not in men but in women themselves. The reasoning is simple – while the perfect man is busy looking for that delicate, feminine, woman who will be awed by their brute strength, and intelligence – a smart woman will be busy perfecting the art of being suitably awed by said brute strength and intelligence.

Now women can help reinforce this notion in one of two ways – they can do so by verbally expressing their awe and gratitude, in a contrived situation where the man is given to think he is 'helping' the woman, or they can do so non-verbally, by making their attraction and willingness obvious, but simultaneously retaining enough mystery that the man is forced to approach her.

In case of verbal communication, the woman needs to be careful to ensure she comes off as amiable and likeable, a notion that is discussed further in Chapter 3, for now, let's focus on the non-verbal cues that they will need to work on.

Now, keep in mind that non-verbal cues, rely for the most part on eye contact and body gestures. Say you are at a bar, and you see a cute guy – instead of going up and approaching him, pander to his alpha-side. Make eye-contact, don't be obvious about it, but let him know that you were and are interested, a shy smile coupled with a soft tinkling laugh as you turn back to your friends may sound cliché, but it works!

The other thing that is of equal importance is body language. A lot of what you are thinking or saying is communicated long before you have ever opened your mouth, which is why you need to relax and make sure you aren't letting your nerves get the best of you. Normally when we see someone we like, we tend to be more physically approachable, our smile comes more readily, our arms are generally at our sides instead of crossed, etc. Often what many people do; however, is they get defensive, and like that boy in fourth grade who pulled on your pig tails because he liked you, we become, guarded, defensive, and unpleasant.

Major no, no!

First impressions matter and you do not want your first impression to be that of a sulky teen. No one is attractive when they appear to be irritated. Think about it, would you want to hit on a guy who looks at you and goes into automatic defensive mode? I didn't think so!

Instead capitalize on your nervousness – shift your defenses and let them work for you. Stop being afraid, or worse, ashamed of your nervousness, let them know that their presence unsettles you; it will only serve to make you more feminine in their eyes!

Chapter 3 - Amiability

The next thing on our how to list, in order to amp up the attractiveness level is actually based on the childhood adage – 'If you can't beat 'em join 'em!'.

Not quite sure what I mean?

Allow me to explain -- do you remember, that female friend all your guy friends had that they didn't really consider a 'female' friend because she was 'one of the guys'? Do you remember how she was somehow always invited to all the 'fun' hangouts and was always in the know – not to mention how at ease guys always happened to be when around her – Yeah, I thought that would ring a bell.

Now listen, we aren't telling you to be that friend. I mean – the entire point is for you to be seen as an attractive 'woman', and not some random tomboy friend they like hanging out with – that is like walking straight into the whole friend-zone scenario – but that does not mean that there isn't a lesson to be learned here. I mean she does basically have an all access pass – what you want to do here is figure out a way to get yourself that all access pass without becoming her.

Now don't panic, we're going to start by simply trying to figure out why all the boys were always so comfortable around her. I mean let's be logical, she's a girl, you're a girl-- and yet there was something about her that men found 'safe' – something that allowed them to be themselves around her. So the question is– what did she have that every other girl didn't?

Well – in order to understand that, Ladies, you first need to understand one teeny-tiny little fact.

We men – are *terrified* of women.

No seriously! I'm not trying to be cute or anything we genuinely are! You just don't make sense to us! I mean ninety percent of the time when you Ladies say one thing, it means something completely different, or worse, when we say something you take it to mean something so radically different from what we intended that we feel like Wylie Coyote on those Sunday morning cartoons.

Girls who have a tendency to mix with guys almost always share one clear and specific trait – they are amiable. They make sense – they are friendly and they mean it, they don't bullshit us and they don't try to hint at things – the verbal lingo is the only lingo – and Ladies, trust me when I say you have no idea how much that one little thing will float a guy's boat!

Now, what do we mean by Amiability you might ask --

Well, for teens it means not picking on male friends for being covered in sweat and hanging out with their dudes. For grownups; however, that same concept can mean something totally different.

Doesn't being a grown up suck sometimes? Argh!

Anyway, coming back to the topic. 'Amiability' for grown-ups isn't about just being cool with men being men, it's about using your ability to be compassionate and your instinctive concern for people to help people and connect with them.

An amiable personality is generally more than just caring and compassionate. Being amiable is in fact what helps you build the bridges of friendship between yourself and those around you. Amiability is about more than just being friendly – it is about being open to being friendly, which is something a lot of young women struggle with. The automatic defenses you have in place are why you can come off as someone others want to be around and want to come back to. Have you ever noticed how there is that one person in the family, or friend group that everyone gravitates toward, and how that person isn't necessarily the patriarch, or the matriarch, but simply the person everyone can open up to? This very trait is what is going to set you apart.

Most men are of the belief that in order to be strong and confident they need to be decisive and unwavering. This cool confident cover is; however, always just that – a cover. And in order to truly be attractive as a woman, beyond your face, you need to be able to get past that cover and show them that you are okay with the man they are on the inside.

Which is why the first step to being amiable -- is quite simply all about being accepting. Don't judge, fuss, or give advice – just hear out what your man is doing or has done or what he wants to do. Be his friend. Not his adviser. In doing so you are showing your prospective significant other that you are a friend.

Once you are a friend you are automatically bumped up in a guys' mind, not only because he now knows that he can open up to you more but also because he will feel safe. He'll feel safe not because of some latent sense of security – but because he will be surer of the lack of judgement that comes along with your amiable nature, which of course is what got him to start talking to begin with.

If you are still confused as to how a personality trait is going to make you more attractive, at least to begin with, think about this, a hot girl at a bar is a dime a dozen.

He'll see you, hit on you, and forget you.

A hot girl at a bar, that he enjoyed talking to, and felt comfortable opening up to – is one in a million. There is no way any guy is not going to come back for more. It's easy enough to be noticed with the right clothes, it's being *liked* and remembered that is key here.

Chapter 4 - Activity

Now that we've dealt with how one needs to be personality-wise, let's talk about the behavioural changes you are going to have to look into. Changing your behaviour may seem like a pretty drastic step to take, just to attract a man, which is why you should think of this part as a life lesson, rather than a lesson in romantic encounters. As a woman, you are about 60% less likely to be half as active as most men.

Shocking isn't it?

That means, while men are out rock-climbing, scuba diving, or engaging in some sort of activity, you are most likely not engaged in, you are basically at home curled up with a chick-flick and a bowl of caramel coated popcorn. Do you know what that means?

That caramel is going straight to your nether regions!

And -

Your prospective Prince Charming is out there waiting to bump into you!

Think of it like this, even if you don't bump into your Prince Charming while you go try out some crazy new activity, you know what you still get to keep? The stories! And believe me, those are some great stories, and great stories are what make great conversation.

Men are ten times more likely to go for a girl they think would match them toe to toe when it comes to fun exhilarating events; they fall for the sense of excitement. In fact, if you are afraid that extreme sports or trying out stuff isn't your thing, opt for non-sporty activities, such as volunteering at a soup kitchen or animal shelter. It gives you those same rich experiences and at the same time you can stay in your comfort zone!

Leading an active lifestyle is about more than just building stories though – regular physical activity is crucial if you want to lead a healthy life. In fact, doctors now claim that physical activity on a regular basis not only helps improve your body and mind but even your sex life!

Don't believe it?

Well believe this – leading an active lifestyle helps boost muscle strength and endurance, it also helps ensure your cardiovascular system is in tiptop shape! It also helps stimulate various brain chemicals like serotonin, which not only leaves you feeling happier and more relaxed, but also has the distinct edge of leaving you with a massive confidence boost, which is always good news in the sex department!

But that's not all ladies!

Regular exercise also has one more super slick advantage to it – studies show that women who are physically active and lead active lifestyles are actually much more likely to have an enhanced sense of arousal – so basically, the sex is better!

However, it is important to keep in mind, that all the activities you engage yourself in to be attractive aren't the only building blocks to your personality. Think of your education for example, what you have chosen to study and what you choose to do with it is also part of your active self. Similarly, the same goes for your career and even your literary preferences. These are all little nougats that added together help formulate you into this interesting person that you actively need to project when you are talking to someone.

Remember, you can be active without being physically active, and while that is also a massive must if you want to lead a great life, even passive forms of activity are something that you need to work into your daily routine and they are just as important!

Chapter 5 - Attractiveness

Now we finally find ourselves coming to the concept all women are closely acquainted with and in equal parts apprehensive and excited about – Attractiveness. Now, while most women are pretty well groomed to begin with, unlike their male counter parts (sorry Ladies!), let's do a quick rundown of what grooming essentials women need to look into or tone down, as well as what dress up do's and don'ts have made it onto our list!

Step One – Grooming

Okay, although it may sound simple – female grooming is one of the trickiest aspects of how attractive men will consider the woman in question. I mean, while on one hand there are men who don't mind a bit of stubble or a grunge hairstyle – there are about twenty more that cannot bear the idea of body hair on a woman or anything other than soft supple skin under their fingers.

Is it unfair? Um, yes!

But once again – *c'est la vie!*

Now the reason I'm pointing that out, Ladies, is because I want you to know that I do acknowledge and accept that because of the entertainment industry, both adult and regular, women are now held to impossible standards of beauty.

I know.

We know.

But we still do get sucked into it -- the same way you do.

Now since I can't change the thought process of the last five generations, I'm going to do what I do best and make you a little cheat sheet. Think of it as a little life hack checklist of the bare minimum necessary to keep a leash on your man – yes I just compared myself to a canine – say what you will but if the shoe fits, right?

Let's start with personal hygiene, now – the ugly truth is, that most women don't actually, bathe or shower daily. Now while that is becoming an increasingly French fad, it is, honestly speaking just gross.

Look – when you are in a relationship – or even if you aren't in one – you need to understand that your body is your temple – so keep it clean – and three-day old body stench is not clean!

Now I know what you are thinking – men don't understand, it's not as easy for us – we have to think about our hair and toweling off, and lotion and blah blah blah - first – stop making excuses for yourself. Instead why don't you try to *help* yourself?

We understand your hair is difficult to manage, if you shower every day, which is why we encourage you to invest in a shower cap.

Shampoo every other day if you have to, but always, always take a shower!

And that's not it – yes we know about your armpit hair issues, and your whole 'I don't want to shave down there' issue – and yes we know exactly how tempting it can be to just leave things to nature and allow it to grow out. Unfortunately, it is massively gross for us. If your issue is impatience, and you don't like having to do it over and over again – try waxing or laser removal – if your issue is the itchiness, steer away from the blade – and if your issue is you don't have time, just grab a damn razor the next time you go to take a shower – which should be daily.

Remember an attractive woman is a clean woman; remember once a man is turned off by this facet of you, there is nothing that is going to erase that traumatic image from his mind, which is why you need to seriously invest in yourself. Waxing, shaving, whatever you like to do, just make sure you do it!

And ensure you smell good while doing it! I mean, half of the attraction is in how you smell, so make sure, your perfume, or body mist is always stocked, along with your supply of mints!

Step Two – Dress the Part!

Now that we have talked about how important it is to be clean and stench free, let's move on to the how to dress arena. Most women have a tendency to either over dress, or underdress, both of which can amount to fatal fashion gaffes.

You see, while we men may not be able to dress ourselves quite right, we love a woman who is put together. In our minds, a woman's ability to choose the right outfit is like a photographer's ability to pick out the proper lighting. It is something that society simply expects of you and as a result something we expect of you.

Think of it from the standpoint of a primitive, basic instinct; a woman who isn't put together, is seen as incapable and incompetent. It's almost like a job interview – you are perceived as you appear. Similarly, men want a woman who is collected and capable of keeping things under control – that doesn't mean we men want to be bossed around – it's just that we want an equal – a partner. We don't want to have to come home and babysit, we want to come home to a warm hearth and be able to relax – and failing that, at least be able to come home to someone who is capable of sharing our workload. I know this may sound silly, but the way you dress, or carry yourself is how we judge this.

A girl who knows how to dress herself for each circumstance is seen as someone who is adaptable and someone who can adjust to her surroundings. Which sucks, to be absolutely honest, because on the other hand men have it relatively easy. They can pretty much wear casual, or dress pants anywhere and get away with it. Women, on the other hand, need to consider what is the acceptable length, how tight it is, what color it is, if it's too revealing, and if it is too old-fashioned. Whether it is appropriate for the setting, and of course what her partner prefers. It is indeed quite a lot to think about, and even though it can get frustrating; try to keep in mind that your outlook plays a large role in how other people see you, so in the long run it is worth it to take the time to make an effort.

Attraction is without a doubt one of the most crucial elements that come into play when you are considering the opposite sex. Sexual appeal, as well as your social ability to fit in is basically summed up in one quick look, which is why, despite the stigma associated with being particular about your looks abounds, people still are very invested in pubic appearances. To simplify things, just remember, being an attractive female is about more than being a fun person to hang out with. It's about being the *right* person to hang out with, and the right person doesn't wear an evening gown to the bowling alley or sneakers to the Opera!

Chapter 6 - Assertiveness

We are finally down to our last, and perhaps most crucial, trait. Assertiveness. Now, as most of you are probably wondering, why would a man want an assertive female if men are by nature geared to put themselves in the Alpha role – wouldn't a mousey doormat of a woman be more appropriate?

Well, simply put, because men aren't cavemen anymore. I mean, yes there was a time when a strong willed woman was enough to turn a man off, but, not anymore, nowadays many men find assertiveness sexy, provided you are able to strike the balance between assertive and bossy, without crossing over into bossy territory.

And what's crucial for a woman to be attractive – she first has to feel attractive. A meek, mousey woman may be appealing as a submissive – but only sometimes. You need to start this journey by realizing that these 'issues' that you happen to be tackling, and trying to change, aren't about you becoming good enough for some judgemental ass-hat. It's about you building yourself up to be this person who is strong and beautiful inside out – quite literally.

Your confidence, and true acceptance of the woman you are, and the woman you have become, are what will shine through the image of yourself you seek want to build. None of it; however, is going to matter one bit if you don't start by filling that void inside yourself – love yourself. Stop being afraid to express your opinion or explain your needs – if you need to, try changing how you go about it, but don't stop.

The days of women being meek mice cowering in the shade of a banyan tree are long past, the women of today are mothers, workers, students, and friends. And these are the women men of this generation are taught to love. That is not to say there isn't a market for submissive tendencies, simply that such personalities are no longer required as it pertains to what men want in women.

So slap on your hat, and voice your opinions, just as you would with a friend, the days of female subjugation have long past. Just keep in mind that you can't let voicing your opinions turn into a competition – relationships aren't about who wins a fight – you know why?

Because no one ever does. You may 'win' an argument – but you always lose that little chip of respect or love in the eyes of your partner – and if you aren't careful, those little chips can turn into cavernous holes, and before you know it, that entire foundation of your relationship is compromised with so many little problems that you won't know which one to fix first. It's like a house with a leaky roof, or a patient with a hundred and four-degree fever – the fever and the leaks are just symptoms of what is wrong – and ignoring them doesn't make it go away.

Got it?

Great!

Well congratulations! You are now officially in possession of all the little inside tricks of the trade – meaning you now know exactly what you are going to need to do or not do to be that perfect woman that every man dreams about – but what's more important, you are also acquainted with all the little character flaws that you have always wanted to fix about yourself as a person.

In fact, now that you have now gone through all five steps of the makeover process, starting from being assertive, to femininely attractive, you now quite literally are capable of having the world at your feet. Well, the male half of the population at least! So off you go – hold your head high, and your dreams tight, as you become the woman every man dreams of and every woman dreads.

Conclusion

Hey there!

Still with us?

First off, thank you again for downloading the book, "How to Be an Attractive Woman - A Step by Step Method to Becoming Everything a Man Wants and Everything Your Competition Doesn't Want You to Be!"– I hope this book was able to help you effectively learn not only how to shape yourself into the attractive woman you have always been on the inside, but has also taught you how to bring out that inner you, and confidently project that version of you when you go out and about!

Having said that, if you're still confused, and need more in depth dating advice, more behavioural tips, or even just how you want to go about being more feminine or ladylike in terms of how you compose yourself watch out for our next book – "How Be a Lady – What Every Young Lady Needs to Know About Manners and Behaviour!" And if you want some more in depth knowledge on the whole etiquette do's *on* the date-check out "Etiquette – A Guide to the Most Common Etiquette Rules and Social Situations Where Etiquette Matters!" – all available on Amazon Kindle!

The next thing you need to do is to put yourself through each of the five steps, and actually make changes to yourself and your lifestyle so that not only can you be attractive, but so that you can establish yourself as the woman every woman wants to be and every man wants to be with!

Finally, if you enjoyed this book, please take the time to share your thoughts and post a review on Amazon. It would be greatly appreciated!

Thank you and good luck!

Check Out My Other Books!

You will find these books by simply searching for them on Amazon.com

How to behave correctly in any situation where Etiquette matters, without feeling tensed or unnatural!

Get your own copy today and find out how you can improve your relationship with your man and as a result, greatly enhance the quality of your daily life together. Starting today and in to the future!

This book shows you how the way you treat others can make the difference in the opportunities that are available to you. You will learn the habits and traits you have that are keeping you from achieving your dreams.

This book starts by helping you navigate the murky and dark waters of rejection, and its tendency to parasitically take over your life, and then branches out by talking to you about how you can feasibly overcome 'rejection', and start living life on your own terms again.

FREE BONUS!

As a special thank you, I offer you a free

NIEL SCHREIBER'S DREAMS box set.

This box set contains three e-books and one audiobook. The ultimate box set for creating the relationships, love and life you desire!

Get your copy here: **http://bit.ly/bonus_schreiber_cs**

FREE BONUS for all Niel's readers for a limited time.

Greetings from the Lean Stone Publishing Company

We want to thank you so much for reading this book to the end. We are committed to creating life changing books in the Self Help area, such as this one that you just read.

If you liked this book and want to follow us for more information on upcoming book launches, free promotions and special offers, then follow us on Facebook and Twitter!

Sign up for e-mail updates on new releases and free promotions by visiting this link:

http://bit.ly/list_lsp_cs

Like us: **www.facebook.com/leanstonepublishing**

Follow: **@leanstonebooks**

Thank you again for reading to the end, it means the world to us!